Glossary

Arctic
The far north of our planet. It is very cold all year round.

barnacle
A small sea creature with a shell.

fin
Body part that helps an animal swim.

habitat
The kind of place where an animal usually lives.

invertebrates
Animals that don't have a backbone.

pod
A group of whales or dolphins.

prey
An animal that is hunted by another animal for food.

Raintree is an imprint of Capstone Global Library Limited, a company incorporated in England and Wales having its registered office at 264 Banbury Road, Oxford, OX2 7DY – Registered company number: 6695582

www.raintree.co.uk
myorders@raintree.co.uk

Text © Capstone Global Library Limited 2021
The moral rights of the proprietor have been asserted.

All rights reserved. No part of this publication may be reproduced in any form or by any means (including photocopying or storing it in any medium by electronic means and whether or not transiently or incidentally to some other use of this publication) without the written permission of the copyright owner, except in accordance with the provisions of the Copyright, Designs and Patents Act 1988 or under the terms of a licence issued by the Copyright Licensing Agency, Barnard's Inn, 86 Fetter Lane, London, EC4A 1EN (www.cla.co.uk). Applications for the copyright owner's written permission should be addressed to the publisher.

Edited by Arnold Ringstad
Designed by Laura Graphenteen
Original illustrations © Capstone Global Library Limited 202
Originated by Capstone Global Library Ltd
Printed and bound in India

978 1 4747 9351 3 (hardback)
978 1 4747 9692 7 (paperback)

British Library Cataloguing in Publication Data
A full catalogue record for this book is available from the British Library

WEST NORTHAMPTONSHIRE COUNCIL	
60000468608	
Askews & Holts	
BH	

Acknowledgements
We would like to thank the following for permission to reproduce photographs:
Michael Liedtke, 24; Getty Images: Richard Lautens/Toronto Star, 15; iStockphoto: Imgorthand, cover (girl), Poike, 28 (girl); Red Line Editorial: 13; Science Source: Philippe Plailly, 9; Shutterstock Images: Aleksandr Ivasenko, 10, alexandre zveiger, 8, DnG Photography, 22–23, Fotovika, 18–19, Gerain0812, 16, gobini, cover (background), Ihor Biliavskyi, 13 (person, top), LaineN, 20, MaskaRad, 13 (person, front), MilanB, 6, natrot, 13 (wall), Oomka, 28 (background), RichartPhotos, 5, science photo, 11; U.S. Air Force: Tech. Sgt. Michael Holzworth, 26–27. Design elements: Shutterstock.

Every effort has been made to contact copyright holders of material reproduced in this book. Any omissions will be rectified in subsequent printings if notice is given to the publisher.

All the internet addresses (URLs) given in this book were valid at the time of going to press. However, due to the dynamic nature of the internet, some addresses may have changed, or sites may have changed or ceased to exist since publication. While the author and publisher regret any inconvenience this may cause readers, no responsibility for any such changes can be accepted by either the author or the publisher.

CONTENTS

WORDS IN BOLD ARE IN THE GLOSSARY.

CHAPTER ONE

HIDING IN PLAIN SIGHT

Imagine you have a special **cloak**. You pull it out of a suitcase and slip it over your head. Suddenly no one can see you. You're **invisible**. Where will you go? What will you do?

People have made up stories about invisibility for a long time. Stories from long ago told about a helmet of invisibility. The *Lord of the Rings* books told about a magic ring. It made the wearer disappear. In the *Harry Potter* book series, there is a famous invisibility cloak.

A real invisibility cloak may sound impossible. But scientists have worked on making them. So far they can't be slipped on and off like real cloaks. But one day you may have the chance to wear one!

Fans can see the invisibility cloak costume from the *Harry Potter* films in Leavesden, England.

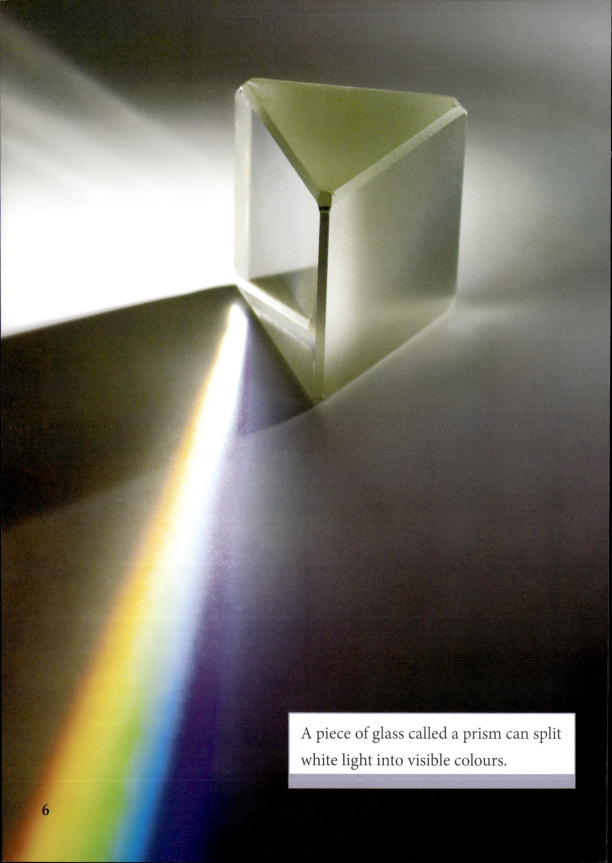

A piece of glass called a prism can split white light into visible colours.

CHAPTER TWO

WHAT IS AN INVISIBILITY CLOAK?

An invisibility cloak is an object that makes another object invisible. It may not always look like a real cloak. To see objects, light is needed. When light hits an object, the object takes in (**absorbs**) some of the light. The rest of the light bounces off. The light that bounces off hits our eyes. This sends a message to our brains. The message tells us what we see. Some types of light are visible to the eye. We see them as colours. Other types can't be seen by human eyes.

To hide an object, an invisibility cloak must work with energy. Energy moves in waves. Light is one type of energy. An object reflects light of the colour that the object appears to be. It absorbs light of all other colours. For example, a green leaf reflects green light while absorbing every other colour. Black objects absorb all light. White objects reflect all light.

FUN FACT

People can make some glass nearly invisible. They add a special coating that keeps light from bouncing off. This glass is used for windscreens, glasses and other products.

Clear glass is almost invisible because it lets light travel all the way through. But glass can't make another object invisible. Invisibility cloaks cannot just absorb all light. They would look black. They also cannot reflect all light. They would look white. Instead the cloak must show the light from behind the object being hidden.

Light can pass easily through some materials such as glass.

A professor talks about a test version of an invisibility cloak.
This cloak shows an image of the background on the cloak.

Scientists have made several types of invisibility cloaks. Some cloaks bend or change light. Some use cameras. None of today's cloaks are like the ones seen in films. In order to make a wearable invisibility cloak, scientists must work through several challenges.

CHAPTER THREE

HOW WOULD INVISIBILITY CLOAKS WORK?

Some invisibility cloaks use **lenses**. Lenses are curved pieces of glass or plastic. They are used in glasses and cameras. Lenses squeeze light together. They can also spread light apart. In a cloaking device, lenses can bend light around an object to hide it.

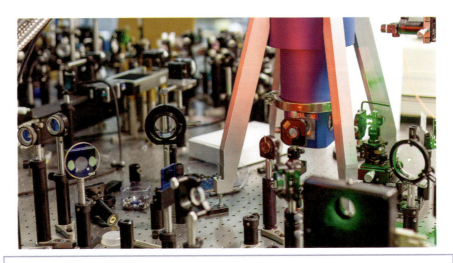

Scientists who study light use many types of lenses and mirrors.

Lenses can bend light in ways that may make invisibility cloaks possible.

11

Simple invisibility cloaks use mirrors. Both magicians and scientists have used mirrors to make things look like they aren't there. Mirrors can bounce light so it goes around an object. If the viewer is in the right place, the object can look invisible.

Some invisibility cloaks use **metamaterials**. These are made by mixing materials. Metamaterials act in ways that are not seen in nature. Some of these materials can bend light waves. They bend the light around a hidden object.

One type of invisibility cloak doesn't bend or bounce light. It copies light instead. It uses a camera to record the background behind the object that will be hidden. Then a screen is placed in front of the hidden object. The screen shows the background. It looks like nothing is there.

HIDING OBJECTS WITH MIRRORS

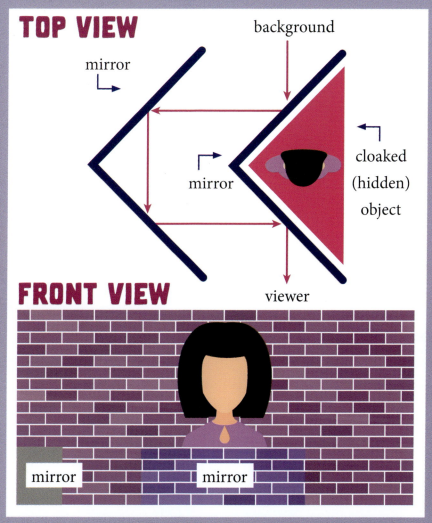

Two L-shaped mirrors can hide something from view. They are set up between the viewer and the background. In this diagram, a person stands next to one of these mirrors. The mirrors bounce an image of the background around the person. To the viewer, part of the person appears invisible.

CHAPTER FOUR

CURRENT TECH

Today's technology has allowed scientists to make a few types of cloaks. In 2006, scientists tried a test with metamaterials. They made a cloak 13 centimetres (5 inches) across. It bent waves of energy around a piece of metal.

But the cloak had one problem. The material could only bend some types of energy waves. It did not bend the light waves that people see. People could still see the piece of metal. It only looked invisible to machines that see certain types of energy waves. Still, the test was a good first step.

Scientists continued to make advances. They found ways to bend light people can see. In 2007, scientists made a material that bent red light. Other scientists have made one that can bend blue-green light.

Two scientists created a cloak that hides objects from being seen by machines that see some kinds of energy waves.

In 2013, scientists made a very thin metamaterial cloak. Unlike past cloaks, this one could wrap around objects. But it still did not work with energy waves that people can see. It could only hide objects from machines that see certain energy waves.

Scientists have used cameras to make simple invisibility cloaks.

In 2014, scientists made an invisibility cloak using lenses. They called it a Rochester Cloak. The lenses took light from one side of the cloak and formed it into a narrow beam. On the other side, a lens spread the light out again. Objects can hide between the lenses as long as they do not cover the narrow beam.

Two years later, scientists created the Digital Rochester Cloak. They used a camera and a screen. First a camera took pictures of the background behind an object. It got pictures from several directions. Then a screen showed what the camera saw. The object was hidden behind the screen. A person looking at the screen just saw the background.

ANIMAL INVISIBILITY

The bodies of some animals are like invisibility cloaks. Glass octopuses have clear skin. All you can see are their eyes and guts. Cuttlefish skin can change colour to look like the seabed. These coverings help sea creatures to hide from animals that might attack them.

In 2018, scientists tried a new idea. They sent light through an object rather than around it. They called it a spectral cloak. To show how it worked, they shone light towards an object that allows some light to pass through it. The light first passed through a device that changed the colour of the light. Then the light passed through the object. On the other side, a filter changed the light back to its original colour. The light seemed to shine through as if the object was not there. This may be one step on the way to invisibility cloaks.

Filters change the light that passes through them. Special filters may make invisibility cloaks possible.

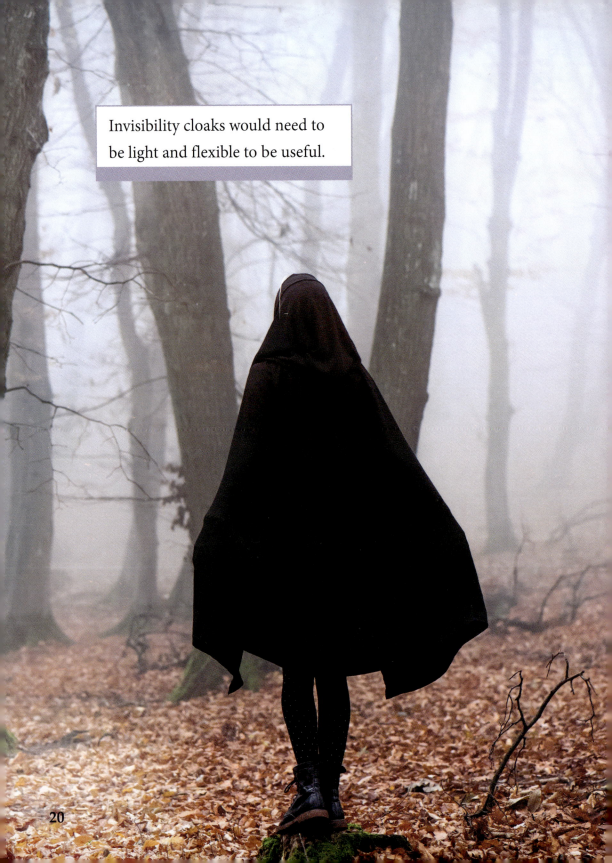

Invisibility cloaks would need to be light and flexible to be useful.

CHAPTER FIVE

WHAT TECH IS NEEDED?

Scientists still haven't made a true invisibility cloak that a person could wear. All the current tech has limits. Some cloaks only work when a person looks at them from certain directions. Other cloaks do not work with the type of energy waves that people see. Many are stiff. Some are hard to move.

To make a true invisibility cloak, scientists must solve a few big challenges. The cloak needs to be thin and light. It needs to be flexible. At the same time, it must cover a large area. It must work from all directions. It needs to work with the types of energy waves that people see.

One day scientists may be able to hide large objects such as bicycles. But they would also need to hide the shadows from the objects.

Scientists have made very thin cloaks out of metamaterial. Some can be wrapped around very small objects to hide them. So far these cloaks have only hidden tiny objects. Scientists think this may not work for something as large as a person.

If scientists find a way around the size problem, there is still another challenge to solve. The hidden object still makes a shadow. Scientists need to find some way to stop this. Then the object will truly be invisible.

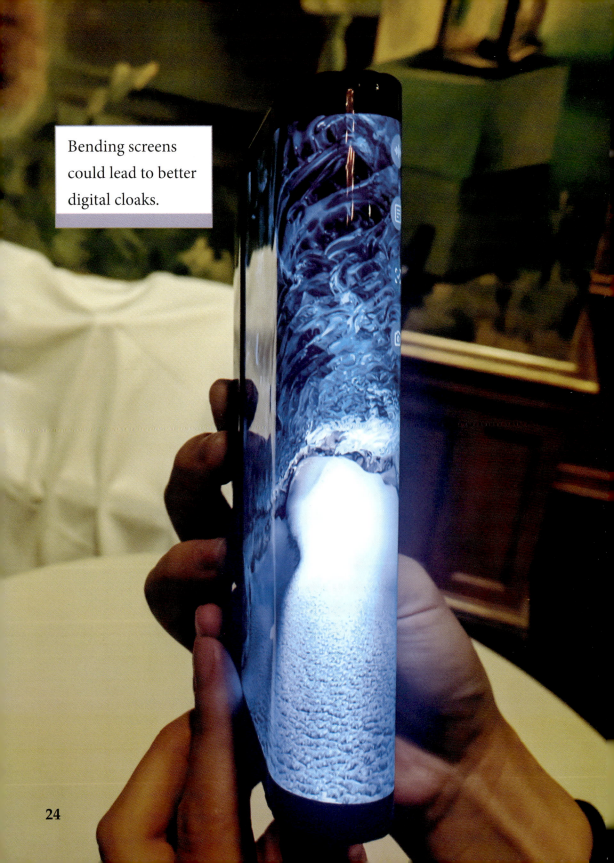

Bending screens could lead to better digital cloaks.

Digital cloaks work with all the light people can see. However, the current tech only works from a few directions. A full invisibility cloak needs to hide an object from all directions. Some digital screens can bend. They might be able to wrap around an object. That could hide an object from more directions. A better digital cloak could use more cameras to record from more angles.

Spectral cloaks show promise. Scientists have proved they work in one direction with a green beam of light. Now they must prove the tech can work from more directions and with more colours. Sunlight is made up of many colours. Making the technology better could allow things to hide in sunlight.

CHAPTER SIX

WHAT COULD THE FUTURE LOOK LIKE?

Invisibility has many uses. The military is especially interested in invisibility. Soldiers could use it to move safely through a battle. Planes and ships could hide from enemies. Spies could use cloaks to sneak up on people.

Invisibility cloaks can have other uses too. Metamaterials might allow surgeons to look into a person's body. Invisibility gloves could help them to see past their hands while operating. A digital invisibility cloak could be used with vehicles. This could help drivers and pilots. They could see all around them. The car or plane walls would not block their view.

Today some jets can hide from devices made to find aeroplanes. Will future planes be invisible to the eye?

Invisibility cloaks may one day go from science fiction to reality!

People once thought invisibility cloaks were impossible. Scientists now think they are possible. We don't yet have cloaks like the ones in films. But it could happen. Scientists are making the technology better. They are looking for new ways to hide objects. One day you may have an invisibility cloak of your very own! What would you do if you could hide in plain sight?

STEALTH PLANES

Stealth planes are planes that people can see, but radar systems cannot. Radar systems use radio waves to find things that are far away. Stealth planes have special shapes. They have special paint. These things make some waves bounce off. They make the plane almost invisible to radar. This means the plane can be hidden from enemies.

GLOSSARY

absorb take something in

cloak loose piece of clothing that usually hangs over the shoulders

invisible not seen

lens curved piece of glass or plastic that bends light in a certain way

metamaterial material that behaves in a way not seen in nature

stealth able to hide from view

FIND OUT MORE

BOOKS

Energy (DKfindout!), Emily Dodd (DK Children, 2018)

Energy (Essential Physical Science),
Louise and Richard Spilsbury (Raintree, 2014)

Light and Sound (Essential Physical Science),
Louise and Richard Spilsbury (Raintree, 2014)

Reflecting Light (Exploring Light),
Louise and Richard Spilsbury (Raintree, 2016)

WEBSITES

www.bbc.co.uk/bitesize/topics/zbssgk7/articles/z2s4xfr
Learn more about light.

www.bbc.co.uk/bitesize/topics/zx339j6/articles/zy3g7p3
Find out more about how to write a science fiction story.

INDEX